MUSIC
IS
EVERYTHING

MUSIC
IS
EVERYTHING

Selected Poems of
SLAVKO MIHALIĆ

Translated by
DASHA C. NISULA

Publishers of Singular
Fiction, Poetry, Nonfiction, Translation, Drama and Graphic Books

Library and Archives Canada Cataloguing in Publication

Title: Music is everything : selected poems of Slavko Mihalić /
    translated by Dasha C. Nisula.
Other titles: Poems. Selections English. 2019 | Selected poetry of
    Slavko Mihalić
Names: Mihalić, Slavko, 1928-2007 author. |
    Nisula, Dasha Čulić, translator.
Description: Translation of selected Croatian poetry. |
    Includes bibliographical references.
Identifiers: Canadiana (print) 2019004814X |
    Canadiana (ebook) 20190048557 | ISBN 9781550968576 (softcover) |
    ISBN 9781550968583 (EPUB) | ISBN 9781550968590 (Kindle) |
    ISBN 9781550968606 (PDF)
Classification: LCC PG1619.23.I45 A2 2019 | DDC 891.8/2154—dc23

Translation Copyright © Dasha Čulić Nisula, 2019
Design and composition, and cover by Michael Callaghan
Typeset in Bembo and Birka fonts at Moons of Jupiter Studios

Published by Exile Editions Ltd ~ www.ExileEditions.com
144483 Southgate Road 14 – GD, Holstein, Ontario, N0G 2A0
Printed and Bound in Canada by Marquis

We gratefully acknowledge the Canada Council for the Arts,
the Government of Canada, the Ontario Arts Council,
and the Ontario Media Development Corporation
for their support toward our publishing activities.

Canadian sales representation:
The Canadian Manda Group, 664 Annette Street,
Toronto ON M6S 2C8 www.mandagroup.com 416 516 0911

North American and international distribution, and U.S. sales:
Independent Publishers Group, 814 North Franklin Street,
Chicago IL 60610 www.ipgbook.com toll free: 1 800 888 4741

For My Family

For My Family

Contents

INTRODUCTION

Born on March 16, 1928, in Karlovac, a city of four rivers in the heart of Croatia, Slavko Mihalić was born on March 16, 1928. Early in his life he was drawn to the arts: music, visual arts, and literature. However, after finishing high school in 1947, he moved to Zagreb, the capital of Croatia, where he soon established himself first as a journalist, then editor, prose writer, anthologist, and a poet. Though the word seemed to have won in the end, the themes of art and music, which vied for his attention throughout his life, are evident in many of his poems.

In addition, one cannot help but become aware of the three distinct locations which have been the focus of his verse: Karlovac, Zagreb and Split, cities which left their significant mark on the life of the poet. These locations are decorated by nature, from trees and plants, to leaves and the grass, birds and crickets and, of course, the rivers and the sea. Slavko Mihalić uses words to draw images and compose a fugue, cantata, madrigal and scherzo of human experiences in verse. He becomes the magician who alone creates a world of words in tunes, uses words to create magic and reveals his passion for the arts, his homeland, human beings, nature, and his native tongue. He presents us with a picture of the human condition of the twentieth century. And these pictures change and transform from season to season, from the very pleasant ones in the summer months, to the very difficult and cold days of winter, under social conditions that may neither be conducive for the survival of a creative individual nor very suitable for human existence.

The topics Mihalić depicts range from love of a human being to love of a parrot, loss of that love and the parrot, war, and a farewell to his own self, as he continues on the road to nonexistence. This road to nonexistence is occupied by a restless modern human being who, along the way, marks the visible and invisible hesitations of everyday existence. Yet in spite of all the threats to life and tragic motifs, this endangered individual proclaims the classic exultation of life, as pointed out by Ivo Frangeš.

During the course of fifty years of creativity, Slavko Mihalić published over twenty collections of poetry, numerous anthologies and translation collections from Slovenian, Czech and Macedonian. He founded and edited journals *Tribina* (*Platform*) and *Književna tribina* (*Literary Platform*), edited *Telegram* and *Most* (*The Bridge*), and was the chief editor of the academic journal *Forum*. His work has been translated into twenty-six world languages, and he has received over twenty literary awards. He made many efforts to promote literature. In the 1950s, while working for Lykos publishing house, he helped found the then Yugoslav Poetry Festival, which was a forerunner to the Struga Poetry Evenings established in the 1960s. In addition, he was instrumental in setting up Zagreb Literary Talks in 1967. In the 1970s, a difficult decade, this dissident poet devoted himself to art and translation. He served at various times as Secretary of the Association of Croatian Writers and as a corresponding member of the Croatian Academy of Sciences and Arts, becoming a full member of the Academy in 1990.

Even with such a productive life and substantial output, not considering only the quantity of work but quality, most critics find it difficult to categorize Slavko Mihalić's work. In fact, very early in his career, Mihalić did not wish to write like everyone else. And, indeed, he never fell into the overuse of symbols and metaphors that dominated the poetic scene in his lifetime. In one of the earliest reviews of his work by Marija Čudina in 1957, she points out the distinguishing clarity of his language and lack of embellishment in the use of symbols. In his work, she writes, Mihalić focuses on his life, and the continuous threat to his existential self, calling his poetry spontaneous, wise, and simple.

Another reviewer, Vlatko Pavletić, who has written extensively about Mihalić's work, points out that Slavko Mihalić did not come early onto the scene with his poems along with the postwar generation. He held back, working on transforming himself and waiting to have a clear understanding of his own self and his relation to reality. Once he came out with mature themes in *Komorna muzika* (*Chamber Music*) in 1954, Pavletlić refers to him as the most lucid post-war Croatian poet who most deeply evokes existential situations in modern Croatian poetry. Pavletić calls him the poet of existence, a human being in a situation.

In his poems Slavko Mihalić does not describe what he observes; he is a participant who depicts a human being in constant danger, alone and threatened, facing life on the one hand and death on the other. The pronoun *I* in his poems is not a confessional *I*, but an archetype of an individual in transformation who writes poems of insight. And, as Pavletić puts it, "Everything Mihalić writes about happened to him and we too experienced it or will experience it." Remaining true to the simple and clear word, reading Slavko Mihalić's poetry helps us ultimately understand the human condition.

Dasha C. Nisula
Kalamazoo, Michigan
Summer, 2018

BOOKS CONSULTED

Benčić Rimay, Tea. *Half a Century of Poetry by Slavko Mihalić /
Pola stoljeća poezije Slavka Mihalića*. Zagreb: Litteris, 2009.

Čudina, Marija. "On Pages of Mihalić's Poetry / Na stranicama
Mihalićeve poezije." Split, *Mogućnosti*, 1959. In *Collected
Poems* by Slavko Mihalić, Zagreb: Naprijed, 1998, pp. 763-
766.

Frangeš, Ivo. Introduction to *Examination of Silence / Ispitivanje
tišine* by Slavko Mihalić Ljubljana – Zagreb: Mladinska
knjiga, 1990.

Pavletić, Vlatko. *A Trap for Generations: Counterpoint of Existence
in the Poetry of Slavko Mihalić / Klopka za naraštaje: Kontra-
punkt egzistencije u poeziji Slavka Mihalića*. Zagreb: Naprijed,
1987.

Stamać, Ante. Introduction to *Poems / Pjesme* by Slavko Mihalić.
Zagreb: Matica hrvatska, 2010.

Šoljan, Antun. Introduction to *Selected Poems / Izabrane pjesme*
by Slavko Mihalić Zagreb: Naprijed, 1988.

Špoljar, Krsto. "Notes on the Author" in *Road to Nonexistence
/ Put u nepostojanje*. Zagreb: Lykos, 1956.

TRANSLATOR'S NOTE

Most of the poems for this selection have been taken from Slavko Mihalić's volume *Collected Poems*, published by Naprijed in Zagreb in 1998. This volume was given to me by the poet himself at one of the Zagreb Talks I attended many years ago. At that time I could not devote myself to the task of translating some one hundred poems. However, in the past two years I am glad I was finally able to return to this project.

There are five poems included here which come from collections published after 1998. One poem is from *Accordion,* published in Zagreb by the Association of Croatian Writers in 2000; four are from *Marsh*, published in Zagreb by Ljevak in 2004. One poem, "The Eye," I pulled out of Slavko Mihalić's collection *Seductive Forest*, published in 1992 by MD. In fact, readers will find in the Contents, appearing in small capitals, the name of each collection with the year of publication in which the various poems first appeared.

One may ask how is it that I have selected one or two poems from one collection and then a dozen or so from another. In fact, after several decades of translating poetry, I realized I have never published a whole book by a particular poet. In translating Slavko Mihalić, I learned why that is. The key lies in one of his poems titled "A Poem Seeks Its Poet." As I was reading and translating it, as well as other poems, I came to an understanding that certain poems speak to me as if they had been waiting for me to translate them. Thus, in response to Slavko Mihalić's poem, I dare to say, the poems I selected for this book have found their translator.

Though it is impossible to render in translation the sound patterns of the original language, with my translation I hold on to the original meaning, while trying to keep as much of the musicality as I can. I made sure the *what* is not lost in translation; however, if the reader detects some of the music in these poems, then the effort has been a success.

Because music is everything since music can do everything.
When music ceases all the magic is only a modest craft.
— "Mozart's Magic Coach" (1990)

COMING ASHORE

for Dubravko and Vladimir

Ships come ashore in different ways:
some violently, with a crash and clatter,
others gently, like a lover.

It all depends on the sailors' mood:
one wonders how was the business.
If the captain had been left without tobacco,
the ship could leap
ashore, up to the store.

It also depends on wives and girlfriends.

And it could happen that the ship docks
very far from shore,
there, in the middle of the ocean,
in some port without captaincy.

SONG OF THE ONE CONDEMNED TO DEATH

I anticipate the day of execution.

They come to me in colourful robes
so strange I cannot feel them
and offer something between air and non-existence.

I wish I were dressed in the robes of some hero,
a conspirator, perhaps, who will be saved
by adventure.

But mainly I don't wish.

Even when the walls assail me with anxiety
and I can't stir big concrete tongues.
I would like them to disappear.

Not so I could wallow in a green meadow,
nor to have a drink of clear water, because there was
        enough of that
but to be released, without a trace, so I don't
        oppress myself.

What else could I wish?
What kind of sitting and viewing position?
How else to uncover my palms?
How else to disarrange my hair?

I expect, they say, death,
but I know that I am no longer and everything is
        superfluous.

EINE KLEINE NACHTMUSIK

That forlornness which cannot cease,
that barking-from-the-leash that responds
    to itself,
that darting by night butterflies with all the hopes,
    but without a purpose;
even the winds are returning with empty hands.

And minor betrayals appear,
persistent filth on feet and hands,
discarded papers, dust and abandoned
    spiderwebs,
footsteps on the street that intend to outlive us.

Only a scream is expected,
the final scream like a shroud for the bathed body,
like a child freeing itself from the mother's
    womb
and like a conductor's baton in the last
    measure of a serenade.

OTHERWISE EVERYTHING WOULD BE MEANINGLESS

They say: people begin to die in the cradle
It seems to me—they rise from the dead
Then live all the more
Eyes open in all colours
Hands then necks and other parts of the body begin to work
In the end time comes for things we call
    the interior
Actually no one has seen them
That doesn't mean they're not there—they hide cleverly
    from the murderers
Life is that little something under the cover of soap bubbles
Go ahead, say nothing
If you blow at it
You'll be a little less wrong
But the dead man will return again
Otherwise everything would be meaningless

THE MOST BEAUTIFUL DAY OF MY LOVE

Today was the most beautiful day of my love.

We walked embraced, but she was not next to me.
I was kissing her lips, but didn't even touch her.

What remains for me now is to sweeten this endless happiness
with a little solitude.

LOVERS' FLIGHT

I'm telling you, we have to leave at once
Where to—we'll decide later
The main thing is to start now
I feel my insides beginning
    to rot

Dried-up eyes hang like burnt
    leaves
The heart's clock is slow—it's barely
    audible
Should I be sorry to leave
    my grave
What can I do if some like it
    there

Let's not linger, my love
To hell with the bags—they're already
    contaminated
But we won't take the road—we may be
    ambushed
We'll go by air—between
    the stars

MY LIFE IS ONLY A PICTURE

My life is only one picture
Some youth with a row of chestnuts in his eye
Exactly when the leaves begin to darken

A smiling face as if before dusk
Which doesn't threaten, only falls quickly
At once from all sides (curtain without sound)

Ceaseless September! Ceaseless dusk!
Here girls go almost in the nude
They ended some very long game

And now move slowly feeling the sweetness
Yes, and in my hand some thin book
Opened but I am not looking at the words

Listening perhaps to what did not happen
Though in me like a past appears
Some silent pain in the corner of my lips

FATE OF A POET, THE MIRACLE WORKER

He fills his heart with all the sorrow of the world.
He could do anything: for example, go beyond
    himself
And extravagantly pour the rain that strengthens
    the insatiable root.
Thus day and night he grew behind himself.

His eyes he made into precious stones for a gift.
He could do anything, dare anything when he tore down
    his own boundaries,
With a hundred hands which harmoniously shift
    in weaving
And in that highest moment
All weave at once.

Endless queues he lets up immediately to
    his side.
He calls all enemies courageous
    in opposition to himself.
He directs nature; thus fills forests
    with tranquility.
Gives river forgetfulness, meadow
    a longing not to finish.

And everything is more beautiful than he,
In everything more desire, strength, reason.
On the wedding day that noble king
    with a crown will be old.

O, fate of a poet, the miracle worker, but only
     until the instant
He gives an ear to others.

AT NIGHT FOOTSTEPS AWAKENED ME

At night footsteps awakened me but didn't pass by
I find my hands near the window in ecstasy
The colour of the sky as if something sublime is happening
The trees truly are much stronger and bolder

It could be love if there were love
But in the world only sleep is left
Some wild vegetation that shuns laws
It's wonderful I am its leaf

Song of mine, be the flower in that freedom
Unrestrained, with a multitude of visible and invisible petals
Like gentle fingers for all deprived sighs

Which call me at night to rescue them
So I take a pen and with a sharp tip open the wounds
Indeed, this what you see is my blood

I BURIED EVERYTHING IN MY HEART

I lost nothing, neither land nor jewels
These white clouds are really wings of angels
—Some gentle handsome men completely resigned
Who don't intend to descend, nor want to love anymore

Golden trumpets without meaning roam between the stars
I am a just man, I never had anything
And no one ever tried to take anything from me
Had I even been? Oh, if I had to, I would have refused

Indescribable light; I even hear white
Wake up, sleeper, to a melted reality

And someone says: soon we'll all burn
First the gods ignited, we will smolder longer

What should I be saving: I buried everything in my heart
And a little more than there really was

YOU, THE SEA

You, the sea, finally someone freed of boundaries
Blue bird, which in a jest becomes black
Relentless righteous one, you still didn't intervene
You let others, as it is superfluous

Bound by the shores which you salvaged
I had seen your face—as it resembles mine
And you'll give my friend a double

So we liberate ourselves from our dense solitude
("Take," you shout, from each theft the more fruitful
But the thief makes only three steps)

Then you begin to rise somewhere where there is no space
Freely, because you are a phantom

The sea! Conquered! which refuses revenge
With a parted bosom always taut

You are priceless and you are perceptive and you are asymmetric
Master of all but the self
That is why I am telling you, to console you

SPLIT

What hands hold you to stand there for so long?
Each street is encountered several times
Some inscriptions, some passageways which are really graves
And so without fear I entered hell and exited

Others remember names, I know shadows
To claim riches there I often failed
But was gently lifted by brotherly sounds
Not to mention the sea, insatiable attractiveness of women

Let me be, you who seek solutions
Tomorrow already I will go by boat to nearby islands
Shaken to the roots by the delight of your wines

City, you are a happy mausoleum
And should someone alive happen by, you will quickly save them
With some passionate death in the middle of a street

BY THE KUPA RIVER SHORE

Right here, at the shore of the blinded river
A whole life passed to return this way
Under the sky with which you finally parted
Broken, it's a wonder you keep assembled
Let's say, one spring day
When everything is grey, erect
And each bird a bird of prey, each stone a blow

Very near the water you can hear its wild beat
As if you came down in front of a door to hell
Each wave some horrible bygone head
Life had been a frenzied gallop
Through trenches that repeat with mockery
Always the same howl, clink, clank

The simplest would be to jump
And wouldn't have I done it long ago
But you are no longer your own, you belong to memories
Which want to burn upon you their holy sacrifices

The water roars, you made a life and it's gone
You are no more than a post to which boats are tied
Only at this place one cannot come to shore

WITH YOU FINALLY COMPLETE

Everything will be written off except love. From its
fire many pale faces blush. Bodies develop their forms.
They go hand in hand, recognized, widening the space of the
world.

Where will you take me, my love? But I'm not
afraid of the steps coming toward me. Neither am I
playful, I only measure my own wish. I dare. All
the roads now belong to me equally. And they need my
courage.

I am speaking to you, love, who are fruitful like the rain,
noble like the evening, luxurious like the sun, who are
always all the more meaningful like the sea.

I am going with you finally complete.

RUSSIAN ROMANCE

Blue lips of autumn
The rain hasn't washed off your bitter taste
Frigid is the bell of a deaf love
A small hut in plundered fields
Black trees on a path over the horizon
Crow's croak, a shot or a cry

Rickety doors of isolation
Each touch of your body a warm bed
The night sings in woollen cloak and deep boots
The wind's whistle rips the road
Smoke descends to the ground and tea
Long passionate prayers

And drops of rain in the eyes
And a dog and wolves in the thicket
And soon dawn

In late autumn
In some book of loneliness

AUTUMN

Carts, if they still pass by these roads, go empty.
Ploughmen had drunk too much sun last summer so they cannot sleep.
They harness horses, hurry out, and only then remember it's done.

Thus you, too, my extinguished love, don't allow me to forget.
With enraged winds pulling off the last leaves
I pass along paths which plead to let them go,
ashamed of their dark eyelids, helpless hands.

But already tomorrow (an hour before the first snow)
rickety carts will be abandoned,
legless horses, as if to invoke, will raise their heads,

drained ploughman will gasp on the bed,

and I already, here, hold a pen, the last candle of my loneliness
and sliding down these lines lower myself to sleep.

A CHORD

Serenity is slipping into me, something like slaughter.

MAY

My young corpse I found among the reeds
It called me in the night exposed among the clouds
I was completely in fragments, broken axle
On a rickety cart near the edge of town

I found my darling meadow with just blooming plums
Not one of my things I could not find
Perhaps I wasn't even absent so I collected myself
Thanks to the passionate May storm

I believe my salvation did not harm anticipated course of time
I only erased myself from some very important lists
Not retracting despair with which I am blessed

In unsparing passion I inhaled feverish fumes
Intoxicated from shamelessness which revived my roots
Took my discernment so I would better serve myself

TUŠKANAC

It happens to everyone from the beginning
(It forgets, so to some it happens more than
    once)
A skilled guide, not a word escapes my lips
Unless words are birds chirping

I sense: it thought for a long time where to place
    the benches
And delighted determined it forgot
    their places
At once a forest and a square where
    magic gently blows
Stubbornness of streets and devotion to adventure

Equally accepts the outcry of summer and bleating
    of snow
And the hungry here always have ripe
    fruits
Like a poet it lends everyone its holy
    voice
Only casually befriends others

And so it grows when it should be falling
My whole heart has overgrown with its
    shadows
Here suicides make friends with frightened
    lovers
With the moon which would here most like
    to descend

A SHORT FUGUE

Neither the rock endured nor the memories
We'll go with wounded butterflies and bent ants
Nor the sky with its famous centuries
Only firmly hold my hand
It's important we endure this night
Or this day, it's all the same, this tearing apart
When not a bird any longer knows its song
Inside your blood boils, your hand is quite cold
Next to us move blind illusions
Our bodies in love will save us
They know only their own laws
Neither river with its sand nor forest
Neither snake already rotten nor the weasel
The sun slants as if against a rope
The moon and the stars as if between the teeth of a beast
Our bed is here among sharp stones
Each kiss of yours a calyx of blood
Never has love been so abundant

FIRST LOVE

I have kept you in my arms
tiny, asleep, still unborn
as you utter my name in a mysterious tongue
while barefoot rain dances between the leaves of grass.

We descend in illusion by those same paths
only the night is no more; azure Korana
illuminated empty shores with laughter;
only sparks are no more.

You are in my arms in horror from kisses
and while the music of May echoes in green scent
between your knees emerges a body of a woman.
We both look at it astonished.

LOVE LETTER

When you were leaving
I didn't know about the jewels
which you left me.
My walks now are full of
happily shaped leaves.
One fountain from the heart of silence
in a rapturous garden
lifts white eyelashes
into my loneliness.
Benches keep moving
down grasslands
toward my footsteps.
How much I could say about
the splits in the sky.
About town squares
always in another place.
In our coffee house
after so many useless years
they again brew coffee.
I look at myself in the mirror
which hangs at your height.
The whole town was erected
in the best place
from old engravings.
Now finally I can say,
I love you.

A SKETCH

Here I would draw a tree
here a hut
but the open sea overwhelms me.
It's putting a white sail in my eye.
I have to listen to the murmur of the waves.
And here I would next to you
sketched
dream in silence
long into the night of the universe.
But all waters always flow
only toward one center.
All the sun rays.
And all calls by fishermen who
cringe in despair.
Here your dress would flutter
and here
in shadow of extended tree branches
glittered a jug of wine.
And only that senseless white sail
borne by the wind
and the last light of the remaining day.

TO A YOUNG LADY POET

No one has yet walked your path
and others cannot help you.
But I hear well how you bang against the doors of caves
which thought only about you.

You will be away for years, there on the other side,
and slowly you will forget about yourself.
When you return, perhaps you will bring us verse
before which we will be helpless.

Don't be mistaken, you will hardly be a mother.
Let your offspring leave you early.
Perhaps you already sense what your purpose is:
in the end all of us will laugh.

Yet something of your femininity touched me,
more like a dream which cannot begin.
So even firmer I applied myself to this unsparing work
which releases small shrill shrieks.

MORNING IN SPLIT'S HARBOUR

How many times in that place. And only once the sea
opened up. Every drop and every grain of sand was in
motion. From the sky light flowed extravagantly from all
sources. How sweetly the walls took it in. Insane
palms almost began to speak. The seagulls were really
flying and the glass in my hand surely inviting. Do you recall
my heart in sweet fever of remembrance: the waves carried
ships with both hands. The smoke enveloped the whole sky and
one could see that it is truly expansive.

Only that one time and never again. All big and
small islands gathered at the margins. My soul swarmed
with a thousand blue bees. And there was not a single stone
that I could not see. Not one patch on the sail
of a boat that for long lies in the voracious belly
of time.

TOWARD THE END OF APRIL

And you don't know you are once again
at the same indecisive place.
But this time there are fewer of those
who expect you.
Yet time is a cleansing
no matter how much one loves sin.
Do you know, invariable rain of forgetfulness.
And to be in spite of everything
a dreamer who doesn't dare.
If only the waters would
truly overtake the shores.
The scent of friendly death
covers the landscape
of your naïve body.
If only they give us the bees
and a butterfly or two.
Damp wind
finally came in.
Isolation
and some other fragile things.
At the end in delirium
I uttered spring.

COMMAND

I had never seen such a white rock.
That's what I was looking for
but didn't even know.
In the field through which no one passes.
In autumn.
We stand one next to the other,
I and the rock,
and seek in the signs of the sky
a command.
We only know
we must
exchange places.

CHRISTMAS NIGHT 1971

I took empty streets
for a walk in the city which in fear
closed its doors.
Christmas tried in vain to enter
with gifts.
Even the taverns turned off the lights
and in darkness drained wine,
sour, fake.
In vain Christmas tried to enter Croatia.
And you waited for me illuminated by hope
that the end of the nightmare is near.

Blessed is
the one who falls under the cross.
We carry ours with much conceit.

IT IS, IT IS TIME

Perhaps it is time
to keep love secret.
It needs to be hidden
in the basement of some deserted
house.
Cut out of flesh,
clothed in beggarly rags.
Close its mouth,
seal its eyes.
Knock it off a cliff,
burn, and its dust
spread to all four
sides.

It is, it is time
when poetry also is a crime.

SONG OF A YOUNG GIRL

In the next two years
I'll desert all of you who love me
who hate me
who don't know I walk beside you all alone
like god who was alone
when he created this tight world.
In the next two years
I'll be sheltered by the sun
and let my swollen body
discover a new sense
of its secret passages.
In the next two years
dear
you will be a melancholy mast
and I a cloud of immeasurable height
continuously in company of hawks
capable of destroying me.
In the next two years
even if on a broom like an evil witch
from above I'll spoil your games
so unworthy.
In the next two years
I who never took a brave step
will be the fateful lightning
for all
who aren't ready for a rebellion;
let their intellect grow dark.
In the next two years
I'll lie perhaps in the shadow of old olive trees
and dream about myself.

In the next two years
those who love me and hate me will search for me
.and those who because of their sorrow
couldn't recognize me
but I'll reside on the other side of the river
in a thicket
with shining eyes
and I'll pray
that no one crosses the river
so that just once I wouldn't have
to make a decision.
In the next two years
(isn't that eternity
which hides its footsteps
the number of its betrayals)
I'll search for myself
because my love was a weak nourishment
because my fidelity was a poor cover
for everything I loved.

A LITTLE DISOBEDIENT POEM

A poem cannot give you more than you have
But it may perhaps disappoint you
It comes to you like an unjust punishment
A poem is a search for one's self
Sometimes you meet someone else
Some woman too insignificant
And you in vain tighten the throat of your poem
Once more you lose
A poem is your sizzle on the fire
But you can say I understood
In fact you recall some subject
Whisper in fever it was in Firenza
And someone else's ridicule means nothing
They also have their wounded poem
While they laugh they don't see it's bleeding
And they push their secret subjects
Small clasps lorgnettes gas masks keys
A poem is instead of what did not happen
Equally so helpless
Yet still there opens some old door
Behind which there is nothing but you recognize the wailing
There are no walls but the windows stand
From which widens a beautiful view into nothingness
From that place you say Homer looked
And conceived so unworthily his Troy
But he was helped by blindness
While I have to continuously look
Choose among poor examples
My God what is it to you in your peacefulness
One little disobedient poem

That twists around my fingers
Is not a poem to you oh God repetition of an old film
Which neither a god can any longer understand
The tempo is really to void
Even though it's about something else
A poem is also revenge
And no one can defend themselves
Only the poet can be hurt
But another will come along and so it is without end

BIRTH OF A POEM

While the poem is arriving
from some mild shift
in depression of the universe
two opposing forces
already vie for the poet's body:
what was and what would like to be.

But when the two
terrible monsters are late!
The poem ignites with ripe passion
in the yielding body of the poet.
And for a moment the whole universe becomes
illuminated with the music of creation.

Illusions you joylessly
test in endless waiting
suddenly become real,
from you to the full care of the universe.
Afterwards the poet lasts a little longer
and only very little

ashes of the poem on paper.

FEBRUARY

This is the worst of all winters: February.
Snows had fallen, northeast wind lies with a pierced heart
among the stakes, and now we are alone with the cold.
People, trees, low to the ground and the sky a broken
window. Winter cuttle releases dark brown colour
and we all swoon around the freezing fireplace.
My soul like stalactite hangs from the lips.
The heart works, works and its clatter strikes
at my ears. Here only a bear from a fairy tale
can endure. O, how welcome is its bloodthirsty
howling. I would most want to rip my own
bowels and lie in a warm womb.
It's February, it has no mercy for anyone.
The earth—a chewed-up bone. No one knows any more
how to light a fire. The sun gambled us off.

A BEAUTY DESCENDS FROM A POSTER

It's autumn
and a beauty descends from a poster
waving her bare breasts.

Everywhere fog and soot.
Beauty very quickly becomes yellow-grey
and strikes in military step.

Naked army pushes through ruins of reason.
Her breasts, belly, the triangle become
law and damnation.
Natives fall like poisoned birds.

What here can the sensibility of a poet do?
He too lies raped in metaphysical mud
and voids in terror.

AN AGING POET

He walks the streets like some ousted god.
Hadn't he created all this:
anger and sadness,
morning city's coughs,
mysterious crimes,
groaning of branches under spring leaves,
autumn carousels of senseless light?

And now,
when on an overpopulated sidewalk
(all these freaks he drew
during nights of fever and hunger)
there isn't room for one of his words,

even when the earth's womb opened,

he returns distressed to his throne,
a grey room without mercy.

Look how his world doesn't intend
to die with him.
Rather it will continue in the imperfection
of some less significant demon.

ARTIST'S SOLILOQUY

You pass the brush
across an empty surface of a face.
It comes to life.
Sends you off with sated mockery.

You pass the brush between the shores.
Whitecaps are your heads.
They drown the ship
in which withers your sensibility.

You pass the brush
over traces of evil.
Blood is found
on your hands.

You pass the brush
over a love dream.
And already posterity, pitiful.
You drink alone in a pub.

You pass the brush
over the sorrow of your wrinkles.
Death selects your colours
covers your grave with the picture.

MASTER, BLOW OUT THE CANDLE

Master, blow out the candle, serious times have come.
Instead, count the stars at night, sigh after youth.
Your disobedient words could bite through the leash.

Plant onions in the garden, cut the wood, clean up the attic.
It's better no one sees your eyes full of wonder.
Such is your craft: you cannot be silent about anything.

If you cannot endure it and one night again pick up a pen,
master, be sensible, don't engage in prophecies.
Try writing down the names of stars.

Times are serious, no one is forgiven anything.
Only clowns know how you can save yourself:
they cry when they feel like laughing and laugh as tears
      distort their faces.

FAREWELL TO ONESELF

Now is the moment for each of us
to go our separate ways: you, legs, follow the footsteps
of which you dream as soon as I lie down;
hands wherever—the left, clumsy, into the parts
of the imagination, the right with the armies; the fingers and toes,
all twenty of them, will go perhaps to some other world;
this one, they think, they've destroyed enough;
after them the ribs, the workers, wounded;
the liver, it's known, will go into the nearest pub (where
the kidneys, the stomach, and the bladder are lapping it up);
the heart will go to the barricade, but without blood,
whispering, so much allotted for love fights;
the lungs between the clouds, the brain into the very sun;
and I will remain alone with this ugly
tongue, created for distinction but it continuously
babbled, got me into the worst situations.
Come on now, tongue, show me what you can do,
now when I am left without anything: fill up the basement,
        the attic, the pantry.

COFFEE CANTATA

Please, coffee, remain
only what you are: morning's first tenderness.
For the incomparability of your colour
and the nobility of the poison with which you revive me,
henceforth do not mention your honorable
origin, hardships on your path to my lips,
secret intentions. As it is, everything that reason
could grasp pales before the equilibrium
which, in one gulp, you establish
in my room. Everything is moving around a single
center, and all is the center, glistening, resounding,
unyielding. Never is time so
in tune with my will as when you, little dark
animal, scrape over the edge
of my entrails. Then, in my own way of hearing,
I conduct the murmur of the treetops under
the windows. But the treetops are no longer there,
and that is what I would not want to lose with continuous
repetition of history, published causes;
the ability to be where one is not,
complete control of things without meaning. With coffee
at our lips we age for all the folly of the world
and feel how sweetly roots burn.

ILICA , WHEN FINALLY DOWN COMES THE RAIN

When finally down comes the rain
It's as if you've come to the banks of a river
And Ilica is some kind of glistening flowing water
Its teeth whitening in the darkness
I am going down Ilica as if staggering over a woman's body
I think we know each other well
When it rains and up go the umbrellas
It's nice we don't have to say anything to each other
There right by Nama store I suddenly become playful
Actually wasteful, invite myself to a glass of wine
While Ilica flows through dusk, that noisy street of mine
Its waterfalls can be heard in the rear of the tavern
Around me only joyful guests
I don't care who is what when I'm off Ilica
When it's raining and dust rises to the roofs
I empty my second glass with someone who all the time
        picks my brain
Tries so hard I could even feel sorry for him
The third I empty with a young man who is continuously on the run
Such are the times, people don't recognize themselves in the mirror
        in the morning
They don't think they'll empty glasses in these taverns
        for long
I return to Ilica and again completely dissolve
We don't say a word, only touch each other gently
We enter one into the other, we do holy things

(1979)

YOU DON'T KNOW HOW TO LOVE, HOW TO HATE,
NOR WOULD YOU KNOW HOW TO KILL

No way to inhale your life.
No way to put together your parts.
In that heap something is always missing,
something continuously slips under my fingers.

I should have left you where I found you,
I should have let you sway in the grasses.
What shall I do with you in this windswept place?
Don't you see we are not of the same kind!

You don't know how to love, how to hate, nor would you know how to kill.
Simply, you belong to some other world
of which, I swear, I know nothing.

You smile at me, and my innards churn.
You call me to yourself, and I see darkness in front of me.
For one of us it's the final hour.

IF YOU WRITE IN THE SAND

If you write in the sand
you mislead the very transience;
the wind disperses your poem
throughout the desert.

If you write in the water
all the dust from your senses
is removed and you can dive
to the very first door of the self;

rescued in a cradle
verse is a game of waves,

secret in the song of fish silence.

If you write in the sky
stars are periods, commas,
chirping of birds continuity of hope,
clouds—a miracle of change.

If you write only with a pencil,
you will have to wait in a ruse
   of restlessness
for the paper to decompose.

And no one will know
what you dreamt.

SPRING ON KVATERNIK SQUARE

You get to the city square, pause a bit.
Again everything changed with one gust of wind.
You hardly believe it, but how not to answer a greeting
    by an acquaintance who shines with satisfaction
yet only the other day dragged like a beaten dog,
    with his little collections of poems.
I produce useful things, he says, those that are
    thrown away upon use.
And as all happy people, he complains about
    the lack of time.
This is probably spring, inspiring time, you think
    looking at the dense stream of passersby.
They keep rolling from one side to the other of Vlaška,
    Maksimirska streets, you suddenly feel released.
Look, here one really only has to believe
and take whatever is first at hand; there will be
    nothing else anyway.
Spring, spring, you carry out your job well, again we'll
    rest for a few days,
get up before dawn and recognize bird songs,
bring sweet disarray into this gloomy time,
again we'll think of love; in spring, after all,
    love is least two-faced,
it takes down everything and sweetly dissolves you
    into pieces.
Perhaps we visit forests, hills, and go after the primordial
    silence
which awaits us from the first day, but many
    reject it,

in fear pluck out of themselves the most precious flower,
silence, which alone re-establishes the equilibrium between
    life and death.
Whoever doesn't return, don't look for them, over there
    footsteps don't echo,
only sink deeper into the origins
    of the universe.

HOMMAGE TO J. S. BACH (1685–1985)

On a plank, on a window,
where the light wove a nest,
so even at night for him the path shines,
in the kitchen, where changes in the time of day
are clearest and at the exact hour
the pot is on the hearth,
with the smell of still warm bread,
milk, apple, with the sound of skirts
which on the clean floor draw
small and large circles of goodness,
with shouts and laughter of all his children,

peeking at times into the yard,
no matter how nearsighted,
where the strange happily mixes with the familiar,
under the quiet order of the world
which still rubs its eyes,
doesn't know, actually, doesn't even suspect,
yet exactly exercises sense,
self-sacrifices with love
and overjoyed finds salvation in the smallest
things, not at all by chance
scattered over the world,

feeling within a wheel of equilibrium
able to measure with the same eye
the essential and inconsequential,
and in pain enduring intense
clairvoyance that doesn't forgive

even reason for its errors, too much in love
with each form of existence,
be it a leaf of grass or a cathedral,
sad as if carrying each coffin
and joyful as if doing
nothing else but create,

nibbling at sudden emptiness,
together with a mouse in a hidden corner,
on bread and cheese and occasional nut,
wrote Johann Sebastian Bach
his preludes, toccatas, and fugues
and other compositions that might be needed
by God and people and the times
outside all time.

AT PARTING

Before you lower the blinds,
before you send things
to the nearest thrift shop,
before you cave in the stones
in the hearth, before you
throw the coat over your back,

walk through the garden and see
how many flowers suddenly gathered,
how sparrows which never leave us
sing at the top of their voices.

Before you drop a few of those
amusing things into your travel bag,
before you in front of the bolted
door break the key,

think, can this landscape
remain in the same place without you,
will it not, when you pull out
all the threads, fall down behind your back?

BY THE SEASHORE

I planted myself by the seashore,
far where everything is in a silver sparkling
and nothing separates, neither the expanse nor time.

Be there, I say, befriend the sea.
It hears you even when it doesn't listen and only rolls the tides.
In the sea is the whole secret of our duplicity.

Forget the fear and approach it more closely.
It holds all its doors open, even for you renegade.
Dive, open the eyes and you will see: here you are more at home.

For days I've been placing myself so unsettled in its proximity.
In the summer and in the winter. The sea never turns off on the inside,
only your blood, heated by the fires, doesn't know.

Don't buy a boat, don't wish for sails.
Day and night sit on the cliff under the splash of waves
until your fins grow once again.

NIGHT WIND

Of the whole night only the wind.
Hairy, black wild boar, werewolf, the last
savage from the cleared forests.
Darts through the streets, presses its forehead
against the window glass.
Again I am in the cradle.

I WALK THROUGH ZRINJEVAC, THE SEA TOUCHES ME

I walk through Zrinjevac, the sea touches me.
I hear the cry of seagulls, murmuring of naked masses.
A ship just docks by the coffee house Splendid.

That's perhaps the sea I carry in my heart
and it calls to the other sea in narrow streets.
It's Sunday; landward breeze ploughs deserted sidewalks.

Soul lighthouses turn on and off.
The joy of unrestrained thought finds places
for the dead and the living.
Finally lost centuries find each other.

The fish utter holy silence.
And even when the sea turns wild,
the meaning doesn't drown.
Sudden storm is a cleansing
of perpetual Croatian sorrow.

The sea touches me and I widely extend
my branches.
Each root begins to tremble
some silvery leaf.
Noon calls from the tower, tide
rises up to the roofs.

We are a big ship of a million
which doesn't intend to retreat.

IN THE MOONLIGHT

Though you know the Moon
is only an ugly, shrivelled tooth
that with devilish precision rotates
around the foamy deserts of the Earth,

though you sense you are so terribly
mortal as if you weren't even
born and that I am only a shadow
of something that departs before

it arrives, yet you are so beautiful
in that ancient moonlight
that one could think

not only are you real
but that the reality of the universe depends
upon, whether you want to be.

CRICKET

Persistent night player,
you perhaps don't know you are the sole
cricket in this silent town
that keeps vigil in the moonlight.

Already seven days
I have listened to your monotonous calls
that gently lull me.
Are you the first or the last?

Will there after you soon
arrive countless swarms of your brothers
or is your call the last song
that still may be heard
in these dark streets
which don't even think about themselves?
That's how my song also wanders
from corner to corner, in doubt,
whether there is anyone who would
open for it a door.

Did you perhaps stray,
like I who don't know
where I could go further?
And if I could,
how to change the world
that is comatose from hatred?

We at least honorably continue
wailing, while others are silent.
Only here and there their heads
sway a little. They no longer believe
either in your chords
or in my words.

They don't know
they only still exist in
our song.

REMEMBRANCE OF RAIN

Of all the rains that poured out of thick
heavenly springs, I remember only one.
And when I listen to others, actually get wet
on slippery streets, here or in some
gloomy North where my soul immediately peeks
out of my shirt, and even in the South, where the rains
are passionate and resonantly bite, in the West
where they drink out of deep mugs and even louder
bang, in the East where rattlesnake rains
dangerously tighten a circle around you, in all those
narrow gaps between the parts of the world,
forbidden places, where thunder
without notice cuts off heads and where something
else might happen, in heavenly
gardens where drops of rain turn
into onyxes, and in hell where the rain
is resinous and hot, I hear only that one
rain, miraculously calm as if there is
nothing else but the rain, your moist
brow and the huge black umbrella of the sky.

BOY WITH A BALL

Look only at your own ball
Not sideways but straight on
Let everything else turn off
Houses that drown or fly to the sky
Morning cries of angry women
Men's rushing with horns, bells

The ball is your new earth
Carefully hit it with your palm
Exactly in the center so it gathers all into one
And flies to the ground exactly as you command
Then it smiles recognizing the game
And returns to the extended hand

Don't think about the hit, it's already in you
It waits to be awakened by two fiery eyes
To be lifted from within intuitively
To grow strong in the hand and land on the ball
Visually always vertically yet a centimetre further
Unwinding in silvery space

Don't listen to the voices around you
In them idles your indecisiveness
Only one incorrect hit: too hard or too soft
Only one hit from the side
And your planet will extinguish
In a puddle, on some sad hearth

This ball is you yourself, your own world
This is you rebounding, this is you returning
Taking down spider threads of boundaries
This is you extending, this is you multiplying
In a game that has no other purpose
Except to play yourself to the end

IN THE SPRING

Time has passed for mathematics.
The man still continues to sit dejected
    at the doorstep.
His wife brings him a glass of wine.
Instead of God, he questions
    himself.

The world is too big to be
    real.
We see ourselves in the mirror.
The man gets up from the doorstep, again
    he forgot everything.
It is spring, wife, we must go
    into the fields.

Who is in the fields, truly stands
    in the universe.
Always asks himself, with what
    to measure something.
The man flies into the sky and the wife
    follows speechlessly.
Whiteness knocks at their temples.

THE FIRST SPRING SHOWER

When the sky pities us once more
When tight doors open up anew
Very little, only for two hours
Orifices which experience doesn't remember
Aren't these white breasts of inspiration?
A smile that is carved into an empty face
    of perfection?
An accidental shift which devilishly
    unwinds backward?

So simple clouds are easily found
So lightenings stroll out of dull loopholes
What was veiled now opens up again
Desire puckers lips for the first three drops
Dust skillfully twirls its lively dance
Nettle immediately turns over its dark leaves
Slither stiff bellies of meadows

I who am mostly a forest, quickly
    rustle
I who am enough a river, flow
    all the quicker
I who am happily a garden, emerge from the
    roots
I who am often a roof, awaken
    all downspouts
Then shout to the chimney to harder
    belch out the smoke
I who am especially a bird, give myself
to the wind that widens the space for the first
    spring shower.

THE WORD

A word is incredible;
so much we instantly
step in form,
to make the same movements
with those we don't understand,
to pass on messages
whose meaning is inaccessible to us,
to never see the sign
that explains us—
but a word, that torch
which illuminates itself
and always is a beginning.

The cry of a child in the universe.
Street sweepers who arrive
from end to end of the galaxy.
Eyes that look at the fireworks
of long extinguished stars.
Renewal of the cosmos
in each grain of dust.

And this, that death
is only an impulse to life,
that faithfully we listen to the voice
which no one had heard,
that nothing is unknown to us
in spite of our lack of knowledge,
that we are most alone with others,
and when we are alone, others are our
sole solace—

But the word, my lady,
which you so carelessly press
between your palates,
one is enough
to darken midday,
one and only enough to
spread the lover's bed at your feet,
the one which raises the dead out of graves
and alone may be death,
to which all might can do nothing
because it is always somewhere else.
A word, whose modest garment are we
and to which we are the greatest delight.

MADRIGAL

Love needs nothing except itself
love of two bones
in the vast abyss of the body
two fingernails of different shape
of which one shrivels and the other spites
two gasping grains of dust
two drops of blood
which have in mind all kinds of tricks

Only love, rustle of two yellow leaves
two flies inebriated with death
two trees which at night without strain
come out of their trunks
two unhappy winds
two boats sunk in the mud
two drops of rain
two letters

Why is your love so restless
Why does your love always want
something else
Why does it incessantly invent trouble
then dreams of love of a fox and rooster
a fish which had enough of the shoal
and a moon which does not wish to shine

A POEM SEEKS ITS POET

Poems are written,
but the poem alone seeks its poet.
Inspired it desires a feast of letters,
with big wondering eyes.

Often it comes upon a timid hand,
a poet who just transports
scrap iron
or gives a talk for frogs.

Often it suffocates, cursing
under the fingers of a verse maker
who measured the world ahead
and now cannot go further.

But the poem does not die.
A poet will break his neck,
with protruding eyes shout in taverns
believing he somewhere by mistake
lost himself.

And while he descends even lower
the poem already tours other gardens,
tastes other thirsty glasses. '

Will it find what it seeks?
Is there a poet for its burning urgency

and has he on time discarded
charms of destiny

to stand unrestrained
under its magic umbrella...

MANDUŠEVAC

They stand in a circle, silently and—see.
Someone descends the stairs and throws a coin
into the water or on a stone in the middle,
then returns or disappears.
A foreigner in town would like to know
what can really be seen, when all is so
visible it need not be seen.
So he too throws a coin and only feels
how his hand, while throwing,
wants to set itself free. He asks himself
in amazement: with what sweet lips did
water touch me, with what
deep eyes did the stone look at me?
And a boy there, who suddenly felt thirsty,
so his strength
doesn't fade, could easily say,
if he were to use proper words:
here is the Passage. On that modest place,
recently dug up for major works
by Manduševac, you can see how
history is only a huge
promenade. And don't be surprised
when you hear the sound of oars: many entered
this way and still many will exit. Here our
dead are as close as a shirt.

(1987)

THE STREET OF CHILDHOOD

Is this truly the place from where I set out
This garden in which I no longer would know how to hide
too large to myself, too obvious and loud
This short street with a soldier in front of the warehouses,
unnoticeable during the day but at night ready for a pursuit
On the other side Kupa in continuous interweaving of waves
Along it trees of linden, chestnut, acacia
which can't seem to harmonize the seasons
Always one puts out leaves too early and the other
still green chatters under the snow
Five-six dilapidated houses which
don't cease to multiply the inhabitants
At times they would only bring out a yellow casket
which would be a wonder because no one seems to be lacking
In the old houses one dies slowly
and time is not the only master
In the courtyard coachmen with weak horses
which above all love cleanliness
If for a crumb in the container they would stop drinking
and be willing to perish from thirst
In contrast to a human for whom life is
above everything and easily renounces decisions
With us were also a few girls with barely
bursting breasts, who knew everything
and wondered at my amazement
Later I would find them in all places, then
when I too found out everything
and could grasp how portentous was
their premature knowledge
Behind the houses day and night the trains rolled

and slowly entered my blood
Then soon I began to think about departure
Oh how huge then the world, and how small now
Around me are all only wasted things
which no longer participate in any kind of game
Only still Kupa runs tired with muddy eyes
and solicits from passersby a glass of clean water

EVENING ON MEDVEŠČAK

Knowledge only distances us from the truth,
because when we finally come to know, on each finger
hangs a skeleton of knowledge, and among them
there is no congruence, indeed: knowledge takes the eye
out of knowledge, and there is no law
to stop the assault.
             Yet, would it not be better
to say: now, when you finally saw it,
nothing else can be seen? Completeness is lacking.
Over there is Mirogoj cemetery, the sun is pouring rosy milk
over it. Here, in front of our eyes,
on Gubčev's Star, two blue trams
violently pass each other; I can imagine how
an unsteady traveller transfers from one onto
the other. In a garden restaurant across the street
tippling goes on among false infidels. The evening passes
barefoot by Medveščak and pales all the more.
             Separated
cold fires of loneliness. And all the more people and things
separate from each other. You see everything
—your eyes swell from the full view—
but nothing of this would you want. You know what is
inside. And you are of the same emptiness.

MOZART'S MAGIC COACH

The earth too is a magic coach, my dear,
look at the flocks of elves that pull it
down dark virgin forests of the universe,
and a witch or two, it's known, would like to diverge it
into a coy ditch, in a passionate embrace.

But there is a coach within the coach, the traveller is a boy
who keeps changing his face, from town to town,
golden or lousy one, from tavern to tavern,
in the forest, among ancient trees
that sing slowly swaying their heads,
on the slopes of fields where wizard ploughmen
pull golden grains from sensual depths
of the earth, from hills to violins and tempestuous timpani.

My dear, Mozart, sometimes he is a coachman,
at times even horses pull the coach skyward,
so frightened winds disperse to all sides
of the Danube, Vltava, and the Rhine,
sometimes a lascivious traveller who drinks the sweetest
wine from woman's lips, from bell-shaped breasts.

Because music is everything since music can do everything.
When music ceases all the magic
is only a modest craft. As shoeing a horse
echoes flutes when the blacksmith is Mozart.
And a jug of wine sings if Mozart's lips
touch the oboe. Rain begins to glisten, footsteps
make sense, hills turn azure, streets
race and curtains are the bare backs of women
when on its own plays Mozart's piano.

QUESTIONS ON BEHALF OF BIRDS

How much do you still believe in a bird
that freely turns in the air? Is there
in our demolished world, any kind
of reason for its existence? Look at the miracle:
it still chirps; had it built a nest
somewhere perhaps? That's what's the most
difficult to take: multiplicity of events.
Simultaneously everything is desolate, not in one
field does sense still grow, but the birds
fly, here and there behind a plastic partition
woodland game peek out without confusion.
Who feeds them, you ask. Or are they only children
of recollection, or does some future time send them
here, in fear of breaking the connection
of events? And whose birds are we:
of the past or future that wishes
to serve fate? With the past we could still
go somewhere, but the future would
need to know that for long none of us
has sung. Long our tongues had been lopped off.

W. A. MOZART

Late at night, during a storm.
Mozart suddenly appeared at the door of the candelabra hall.
He was a savage out of forgotten primeval forests.
He was an oarsman trying to connect two shores.
A sweaty blacksmith he was and a horseman
who carries mysterious messages from sea to sea.
A runaway from prisons whose king's name
is unknown.
A fairly late pilgrim from the Holy Land
with claw wounds from hellish monsters.
A cellarer. Fire-eater. Cobra tamer.
And when he lowered his fingers from the piano keys
no one moved.
All sat lifeless in their chairs
only their eyes shone.
He returned into the stormy night where
his grave is thoughtfully hidden.

GUITARIST

Strumming the guitar he was singing:
"Is there enough air in this song?
Can one see through to the other side?"

THE EYE

The eye comes out of its drawer, it's in a good mood, well
rested, calming powder worked well.

It flies out the window, not quickly as insects do, not even
the slowest ones, but slowly, stately, at first almost half closed.

Because, the eye is aware of its powers. It is hard for the ear,
for example, to prevent piercing sounds from penetrating to its core.
Of course, a person may press palms over ear lobes, and
the ear will not go to court for it. The same person may, after all,
also cover the eye with a black rag. However, we are talking about
free organs.

So among them the freest is precisely the eye: it
can look but not see.

We follow exactly how it does this. It says to itself:
look, but don't see anything. Once assured it can still
do this, it says: and now things very far and vertical. Clearly
it observes a poplar tree on the horizon. Then it tries again: and now
the nearest things, those that are unclear, and that flicker.

You probably know the eye can change colour, lengthen
and shorten the human form, indeed, see what someone else sees,
look behind a wall, contemplate what does not exist.

Sometimes my eye asks me anxiously: does the eye have
the right to choose, to look only at the particular, each small grain itself,
perhaps only a piece of one, or is it its duty to combine all
into the whole?

The same questions also torment me: the whole confused world
or only the particulars.

Duty and enjoyment. I side with my eye: for a small
seed of dust. For imagination which supplements.

The eye returns to its tower, into its delicate drawer.
What is important, everything is still in its place.

(1989)

RAIN ON THE ISLAND OF PAG

The rain goes around the island, lingers. Soaks the vineyard well,
then goes off to the sea, makes circles for a long time, then returns and
sprinkles the sheep. It creeps somewhere into a deserted shepherd's
home, rests a few minutes and then runs down a rough road, raising
dust.

No one complains. Not even the fisherman who sits in a boat
in the middle of the bay. He doesn't look, but asks, do you want a fish?
It, a girl rain, blushes and flies off into the olive garden. So
pale, but already showing signs of womanhood, tries to
climb an old tree, and then becomes sad. It's sorry the olive
trees are so alone.

Unhappily it continues into the village, gets angry at the careless
people and empties out to the end. Not a drop remained.

Behind a cloud the sun peeks out, also wet.

A pleasant scent envelops the whole island.

OPEN MARKET DOLAC

Morning market, a vibrant sparkling of colours, nearby the provinces.

Plays eye roulette.

Slowly one enters festive gardens; there are salad doors and tomato doors. At the lower level stalls, cattle, hogs.

Bluish smell of milk, cream, cheese.

Cathedral bells echo widely, old women enter and exit, God doesn't count them and always one stays.

I am high above Dolac, among grapevines, and I extend an empty glass.

The sun happily fills it.

CONCERT IN NATURE

I let the left leg take a walk by itself. The right thinks for a while, is there a possibility it will desist? Looks at me from under the eye, evaluates.

It probably thought I was only testing it, so it too takes off.

I could have waved to them, but turned sullen. Let's see how far they will go. Actually it is not right they so easily abandon me. Where will we end if each goes its separate way!

First they go through tall grass, lively discussing. I wouldn't say they quarrel. Then they turn into the corn field, where I follow them faintly, and in the end appear on the road.

Of couse, they are returning. After all they are my legs.

I ponder with what face to greet them.

I turn my back.

KARLOVAC TRAIN STATION

Arrived from nowhere, forever standing in that empty
train station, on flat ground, at dawn when the sun cannot yet be seen,
and the birds are the loudest. Buried himself into a part of fate, a seed
that does not think where to go, identical to a plant which does not intend
to grow, deserted from self.

Still happiest in the summer when everything is in swing, opens
up to empty itself out, at the end falls in the midst of festivities.

Maybe I will just move closer to a traveller who is in a rush deathly
afraid to be late for what he was ordered to do. The train which will not
arrive or even more efficiently gets ahead of itself.

Those who know how to cry would have much to do instead of me,
as I admire the expanse of the day that awaits and praises itself. Birds
grow silent, divine sun drags over the sky, the trains roar in eight
directions, and I again wait for dawn, a short moment while the light
appears before the sun.

And to the one who doubts, I say: here a piece of me will remain
completely useless and unseen, which no destructive power can move, I
need nothing, neither water nor air, depend on nothing, and even the sun
itself will once cease its step, equally happy in the silence of the seed to
discover the real absurdity of its movement which interrupts the bliss
of morning twilight.

OPEN MARKET IN SPLIT

I sense you are among that multitude running confusingly in all directions, buying, selling, uttering uncommon words, giving vent to most insolent impulses. Drowned among watermelons, fish. I know you wave angrily with your arms, maybe you have six of them like the Indian goddess, you're a bit man, isn't it, a bit woman, trying to outsmart the sellers and you can hardly restrain yourself not to turn over the bench full of figs, apples, plums.

I stand on the side and fear the thought I might have to follow you.

How can I find you in this whirlpool? Now you hardly resemble yourself, and I don't want any of these items, all are full of someone else's touch.

I will look for you when all leave. This afternoon? Tonight?

You will be sitting in the middle of the market among the refuse.

Again, inconsolable you.

SCHERZO

In a prophecy by a fool the stars majestically
descend to the earth. Now they sit already at each table.

You will see, time will come, when angry housewives
will sweep them off the threshold with a broom.

We still have not seen an intoxicated star. But soon when meteors
arrive, anything may happen.

Do you miss peaceful afternoons in grass by the riverside?
Ah, flies!

In the future, near our ears will buzz all those cosmic
vagrants, planets, comets and we will have to move on again.

CHRISTMAS 1991

Christmas Eve, silence in the manger.
If they were people, I would say time
standstill is natural on this night. Or all
are in the grip of wailing sirens, the first
explosions of grenades that again fall on the city.
But no, these are only pieces of wood cut out
by clumsy farmers' hands: Jesus, Mary, Joseph,
Three Wise Men, shepherds with herds, a few
angels up high attached to the ceiling.
One cannot say they are dying of fear.
They only speechlessly watch our
sadness, and powerlessness, big emptiness in the room
around the Christmas tree, forlornness of apples,
figs for which no one extends a hand.
I feel even the candle doesn't want to light.
And in that silence, in that stillness, I know well
someone will begin to speak. A tree in the manger
will begin my cry and tonight after all
will be Christmas.

RAIN

Spring rain, palms open up and
close like the leaves of a water lily, full of butterfly storehouses,
waiting.

Thunder hangs over the village bell.

Old women in tiny steps scurry, invoking
the dead.

The happy ones sit in a tavern, their glasses empty,
singing loudly but nothing can be heard.

Let the rain fall, let it fall for days,
years, perhaps the world will become round.

THE KING OF MIRRORS

How many lives does a human being have,
appears into how many different mirrors?
In the first, loves and attempts to forget.
In the second, seriously tests isolation.
In the third, howls beyond the city walls.
Still somehow keeps intact.
Doesn't even suspect when crossing the street
into what nets he entangled
or what all he broke.
If he knew, he wouldn't enter through any door.
Wouldn't leave his room.
Wouldn't even think because a thought is the first shout.

Did you ever speak to the end of your throat?
And every word has a hundred dangerous meanings
if another gets closer to it
whether it wants to or not.
Where do all uttered letters go?
Some immediately dissolve, but don't think it's the end.
Others bowed retreat down steep passages.
Third know well what they do and superciliously expand.

NIGHT SONG

Night is a celebration of silences.
Everyone rises a little from their
    place
and hears oneself ask: is it the hour?
The answer one knows from long ago but happily
    listens.
It's similar to the murmur of treetops.

In the night all find their own shape.
Thus at first dusk a burglar's
    fingers spin.
A holy man converses on equal footing
    with God.
A vagrant wants to go still farther
    from himself.
A drunkard in wine seeks his younger
    face.

In the night everyone has a straight path
    to the stars.
Many do not return and wonder
    why earth is not
    lighter.
As if someone measured a vision
    floating in solar eclipse.
In search of a voice out of the depths.

MAGICIAN

He works at night silently in a dark room
which travels when the doors are firmly shut.
Not a boat nor a rocket can reach that
far, not one snail can so enter into itself

as he and his room full of old things.
And they also change, stretch like
a balloon, spark, chirp, hiss, get bigger
or smaller accompanied by the soft organ of his

laughter. He writes out long sheets of paper,
mutters into his beard and already he and the room
move from the place, then suddenly race
among the surrounding stars. They sway, he sings

as if he had drunk wine and doesn't even look
through the window. He was creating all this
at the table. And the tiny seed of dust
into which he and the room enter, from an unknown

direction. Perhaps from the very core of the idea,
dizzy thoughts that circulate around him,
and which catch him, the master magician,
in a trap out of which he painfully pulls himself out

into reality. With effort he gathers all his
pieces, but the most pain gives him
the soul which resists returning
into the cage. It's morning. Drowsy he opens

the door and stretches at the threshold as if he had
slept for a long time. He yawns. Waves his hand.
Indeed, the world is, thank God, intact
and doesn't suspect that last night he was again

at the edge of chaos. The mail carrier, chimney sweeper,
police patrol pass by and in vain secretly ask themselves,
what does this man do? Repairs
shoes, watches, mixes grasses? Or in fact

does nothing, as they say, and
lives on charity the city sends him
from time to time? And they don't even
think someone respectable in this land

could live off writing no matter how it is.
That the whole world is in his
hands and that it depends upon them a little
into what the writer will turn it.

LAMP

At night a little tremulous light leads me into the meadows.
Hot air chokes me, every hour I lap up.
I am not afraid, only I don't see the hand that carries the lamp.
What should I say: is it there or not?
Someone is looking at me, curiously, waiting for me
to speak.
But I know all this will last only until I utter
a rude thought.
Then all the stars from the sky will descend upon me.

A POEM

If a poem is a bird, stop
And if it's a butterfly or lightning
It would most like to be a soft June rain
That takes dust off the feet
Quietly whispers to the bones
It's not remembered but it cannot be erased
A poem tied to all parts of the body
Wisdom of ancient oracles
Which is a blessing of our ardent wanderings
If you break it up, the poem can always
Be put together again
Solemn isolation of the spider
Not the one with a helmet
Drawn on posters of flies
With tanks of caterpillars
Planes of wild eagles
I converse with the sparrows as with myself
That much I am afraid

PANIC

There is no explanation, all shows are cancelled
The wind dropped to the ground and sniffs last year's leaves
From the view the seasons have disappeared
Day and night, hand in hand, go toward the cemetery
Women hurriedly prepare suitcases
Things are nervous, pushing fingers away from them
Don't fear, no one will recognize you
You can easily hide in the crowd that pales
Jump over a paper wall, run across the empty river
Man and dog stand, above them the sky splits
An old woman passes by: she is either blind or sees through you
What does she want? Where is she from? She does not answer...
You can recognize her face, take her as one of yours
Soon you will have no one, you will be nothing yourself
There is no explanation, all shows are cancelled

NO MATTER WHAT THAT MEANS

Yes, to leave one's house,
take a well-packed bag
of crumbs, then, when the mind
muddles, drop from it grains of bread
and know you can return
and raise tired walls
or sit on the foundation and yourself be the wall,

but it's different when predators come
and throw you out into the cold night,
because they want your bed,
your table, chair, towel and pitcher.

They blind you so you will not return.
They make you deaf so you will not hear the blue bird
which notifies you when the grain is ripe
and who loves you in the big world.

You know they will never find the thin threads
that raise temples, will not know the magic
words which open the doors, windows,
even more secret doors that lead into the sanctuary of the house,
and that deer will never come close to them
with which one needs to converse so the forest
will put forth leaves and the snow will fall on time.

But for you, too, the bridges are destroyed,
wooden Christs on crosses are pierced
to blood, all roads dug up
so you easily fall into a trap.

Your town can no longer be recognized
neither in heaven nor on earth, and you must
continually go toward the light, no matter what that means.

MORNING IN KARLOVAC

An old woman opens the attic window, lifts
herself up, her hands entangled in the curtains,
she feels the room will fall down her body,
unhappy heavy hands don't listen,
throw themselves into the fresh air, immediately
I recognize the fisherman who sits in a boat,
morning sun warms his right side,
he does not intend to move,
sparrows and children romp at the shore, dust
rises up to her home, then
slowly descends to the river, three
soldiers pass by, girls run out of a doorway,
waving their purses, sacks, net-bags,
above them rises a dreadful mushroom of light.

WORDS BETWEEN US

Words between us
are poisoned hornets that prick
our soul. No sooner a voice flies from another's mouth,
our subconscious, though we know not,
tightens into a cramp, despair, the body in defence
from the attacker utters its own
wicked word. We speak, and all the more
are wounded. What else can we learn
one from the other, except in panic
gnaw at the same tasteless flatbread? Quickly
we are becoming deathlike.
         A small remedy for us are
words of love. But who really knows how to utter
them? The most beautiful ones, they are silent,
tenderly embrace the bones, flesh, bring
faith to the conscious, arrest time.
They are rarer than gold, so in vain
we seek them, dig up even higher hills.
No, they come of their own, when they sense
open space in our soul to which
they descend from the beyond.

OLIVE TREES

At night olive trees take off their roots
like you cross one leg over the other
before a dance, and hurry down southern stormy
plains, our mothers, sisters, women, lovers,
large female folk to whom at dusk,
under the starry sky and mirrors of the Moon
a broken thought once again comes to mind.

Really, in daytime olive trees are no longer in the same
place. And whoever is stubborn and wants to see
that which is not, like a madman who uncovers
the curtain on the unreal world, could hear
a mocking laughter. Other olive trees are
in the field, other women are among us.

Where did they go those whom we
once saw, loved, and rushing
remember only their likeness?
The question, as always, guesses both ways:
neither are we the same. In daytime we, in man's
dream, ran off to impassable forests.

WHO AM I AND AM I

Forever I've been writing this letter
and when I don't write and only listen
will there from afar or near appear a voice
I forget and go down a hidden path
which brings me to wide city squares
where there's no one and again I remember the letter
which speaks to someone in unclear words
and mysterious whispers underneath them.

Life is a quiet fire in contrast to a strong flame.
As soon as you write out the first line it already goes out
so you again attempt to light it, you or another hand
that slowly pulls itself out of your ashes.

You don't know into what madness the letter went,
Did it at the end make sense or did it go with the wind?
It doesn't wish to say anything about that
but writes, at night rapidly breaks into sleep
so I no longer know who am I and am I.

PEOPLE WHO SING

People who sing
Arrived from caves, skyscrapers, under bridges
Stand above the earth's threshold
With their mouths in a smile
Voices bursting out of all positions of the body

Illuminated forms that inspiringly grow
See beyond allowed borders and sing
not knowing they exist; they dream with open eyes
Sense themselves pulled out of hospital beds
From courthouses, prisons, in front of the wall
Of destroyed schoolrooms

They run down mowed streets
Stand behind a counter in a store of flower airing
Guide plump children through blissful labyrinth
They were tyrannical husbands and malicious women

Who stand at the top of the hill of humanity
A thousand organ pipes that turn into ploughed harmony
Into a song of triumph, which is the key to human existence
The one that laps up, yelling, while for it children are born
It rises above the horizon and opens heavenly doors
Plants forests which still haven't gained freedom
Cries over a dead river and returns its green spring well
Writes verse, acts in the city square, paints under the sun's storm

The song that does not cease even when the singers disappear
It can be heard incessantly clear above golden deserts
And their mouths can be seen—only it's not known to whom they belong

RETURN TO THE SEA

It's time, start toward the glittering shore
There where the swimmers left skin, soles,
    fish bones
And where the northeast wind extravagantly spins in the air
The sea waves suddenly turn dark, foaming

Go barefoot through the carnivorous bushes on your
    short pilgrimage
And let no one see you, let no one feel sorry
    for you
Don't rush, stop a moment in the swarm
    of hornets
You know there is no purpose in shortening the path: it lasts
    longer the more you rub it out

Perhaps you will reach the coast in late autumn
Or in winter, to try lashes of the wind
Your blood will redden the snow and ice and you will
    break
Joyful in the understanding you endured
    your measure
And you did not beg for mercy at intractable city squares

Icy are the teeth of the sea for the remains of your skeleton

APRIL TICKLES MY TONGUE

April tickles my tongue.
Sits with the wind at the Easter table
—both with happy heads—
and without a word, deeply affected.
At the window glittering rain chatters.
In the sky the sun lights up the stove.

Easter plants a cross into everyone,
that is why April is so benevolent.
It unfolds multiple colours, more fragrances.
The grass like a lover glides over the meadows.
The cross seeks the quietest place in the soul.

—I know spring is coming
when the last snow, ruffled
but already wet, falls into the cup of lilacs,
and the stork, upon return, spreads its wings
over the tired world,
full of blooming hope.

April stretched between March and May,
unreliable out of its great goodness,
from the clouds that gather into a storm
and the young sun which tastes every cup.
It tickles my tongue, wants me to speak,
but I am silent in a high temple
and let the words write themselves.

MY SOUL IS FULL OF ANCIENT TREES

My soul is full of ancient trees
which roam the fields, hills.
They don't notice me but I hear them
when they raise a dark voice in the wind
or are silent and only a twitter of leaves can be heard
as they move from the top to the lowest branches,
and the birds peek out of their blue doors.
I do not know who all lives in a tree,
who hides during the day in the tree tops
and at night walks with a glowing eye.
Who in the silence knocks under the bark,
who is deep down in the earth with the root.
Trees are not from here like no one is
from this aged, coarse surface.
They came to freedom but are pursued,
beaten, cut with axes, a saw, dynamite.
In the summer, I sit fragile in their silence,
on that final shore of inhumane sea
and know that I am no longer alone even though hands
do not extend to save me. Someone watches and ponders
whether to open for me the door.

TWILIGHT PROMENADE

Trees in sleepy rows
From the gardens a blackbird flies to an empty branch.
From Korana the fog drags; will it bring someone?
Stillness of late autumn knows all hollow answers.
Nevertheless I wait, decomposing.
Heaps of fallen leaves, dead grass.
It doesn't bother the blackbird to seek in vain.
I could tell you I stopped halfway
and know not what I covered, that I cannot any more.
Distant sighs of twilight Karlovac.
The bell gives a sign, small bells fly into the air.
On the promenade silver dust.
Softly I touch a broken bench.
In the houses light goes on, shadows rise.
The path leads into the stickly darkness.
That's how written pages separate.
Still one must persevere, those you wait for will come,
look, see a blank glance, wave off.
Only blackbird, on Earth, turns over muddy leaves.
Own shadow, I remember its song
penetrating heavy chests of forgetfulness.

POETS

They are here, between the walls.
Who mentions them, speaks of the dead.
The living frequent pubs and are nameless.
Here somewhere they live in a word which continually
     changes its meaning.
It catches on fire and becomes for them an enamored
     lamp.
Word is also a pen which shakes off its
     dark feathers.

God, without their knowing, helps them to survive
And look: with a few pennies in a shallow pocket
they raise palaces in tight passages
that allow only them to be led
     into exile
from the world which does not even want to exist.
Indeed, there is nothing except their
     verse

which terribly anger God and he shouts
     at them.
They smile because at least someone reads them.
The Creator, sad, collects after them
     papers
and when he is no longer angry, reads them to the angels
who are amazed by the poets even though
     they understand nothing
and praise the greatness of God's miracle.

THE MUSIC OF ROOTS

Night extends for hours.
I entered into its warm den,
opened up the shirts, coats and
sprawled into the music of roots.
Out of nothing pulled long threads
of joy, spoke with the people of insects.

GLAGOLITIC SCRIPT

Folds trees into herbariums
with closed eyes, widening nostrils.
It is summer, abundant, tries to leave a trace
on the skin of the innocent earth,
would it not, though sinful, conceive.
Napping wind, midday sleepwalker,
writes out sonorous Glagolitic script
invoking rain.

IN THE SNOW

Lost in the snow
doors, water wells, haystacks.
If you see a house, it has no roof.
There exists a muffled music of winter
which at sunset migrates toward the horizon.
The moon with its teeth cracks the glass of the windows.

FINGERS OF WAR

War knocks at the door of the old castle,
then at the window of the rooftop
but there is no one.

Is war only an angry index finger
with a helmet, a halter belt?

By itself the oil lamp lights up.

SOLITUDE

By the burning stove the walls
again close into a shell.
Outside snow—everywhere only tenors—
lowers the sky to the windows.

I knock at my own door, from the inside.

GENTLE KNOCKING

Is autumn at the door?
It's not here yet, but its gentle
knocking can be heard everywhere.
By this discreet sign, sneaking,
I become a conspirator at my own door.

—Is it time to put things in order?
—They depart on their own, rival, leap.

I remain with the clouds, the leaves.
In the autumn wind I smell a nice trail
and roast with tame chestnuts.

A STEP – A TINY STEP

In walking a step stalls.
Hangs in the air, attempts to know,
and returns.
No one can hold back a return.
A step returns into a deer's leap.
There is no more deer, it returns to its fear.
Into the beginning of a beginning it returns, reads the genes,
Now smaller jumps through the fields.
Meets a grasshopper that kisses it in the knee.

THE LAST WORD OF LOVE

In a hospital, in a foreign land.
Was it not fate that two former lovers
meet as elderly in a packed waiting room
in front of the doctor's door?
She sees nothing even with glasses,
he cannot sit down from pain in the hip.
He thinks, what were their last words long ago?
She entered first to see the doctor and did not return.
He framed the final word
and left the hospital healed.

DEPTHS

More often I listen to unknown depths
that rumble in me and around me.
Deeper than the deepest earth's
abyss. Tempting dark whirls
of the universe, loud, still unseen
by the human eye
canals that lead through us,
gigantic yet still narrow arteries whose
beat we sickly hear in the nights,
so we only here-there hear them or it only
seems to us that we feel destructive
laughter which immediately departs our hearing
and understanding. The earth is too small
for reason that poses for us dizzy questions
—our reason or a tiny part of enduring
brain, enlightened, on fire, too
burdened to know us.
We can only hear, and who really
hears and understands, who convinces oneself
of knowing, feels immeasurable joy
even though the step brings one to
the edge and shatters the very self?

GRASS

Instead of letters, the grass which grows
by the curb, you don't see the difference between
its leaves, but together make sense that doesn't
interrupt. The world opens or closes as soon as
you speak. But, look, grass is in
the world, it doesn't even listen to people's speech,
it's closer to a smile than continuous cry,
it sees by what it is, capable
to spring from its own ashes. What a
signpost in each season is the green and yellow
grass! Immediately your view opens up and things
seem more real. How brightly it calls from under
the snow. It chirps fiddle-bow of sleeping
crickets. Again it elicits on your lip
a word, hard, humane, which only
can ring a little with incisor joy.
It doesn't last long just as snow
isn't lasting. Haymakers tread. Drunk.
Intoxicated by the grass which smells of armpit
      freshness.

AUGUST, SEPTEMBER

All are now preparing suitcases, putting on suits,
missing parts of their bodies that remained in the sea,
at the seashore, during July nights among the shrubs,
deck chairs. They were nameless but now are called
by their names. A strict guard appears
gives them a fine for their lost souls
and immediately chases them out of the borrowed heaven
into the chaos of roads that run in all directions.
                                                    It is August,
summer is approaching a heavy bill. With a dark
smile speaks of the barking wind that creeps
between the trees, of drooping tips of grass
and leaves that are learning to fly. Time has come
for stiff shirts and rancid coats. Fog
pulls out of the pocket moist handkerchiefs. At the exchange
September devalues gold. The sea retreats
into the depths.

THE END OF A SONG IS ITS BEGINNING

The end of a song is its beginning
in another voice in the same window
in which singers await their turn
not knowing for themselves, frozen in darkness,
while light seeks new sturdy mouths,
slowly, letting the wild shout to their content
then disappear into the forest in a race of wild pigs,
leaving the helpless to destroy the sky above them
thinking it is only a thin doormat.

Here again the light glows red on new lips.
The voice reverberates around which the Creator
draws a body, writes for it a shorter biography.
The light disappears. In darkness a funeral procession passes.
Then a few mouths beam. A quartet. An octet.
The harmony unites the sky and the earth. The organ
expands its sonorous lungs. Darkness. Light.
Faces are not remembered, only the song lasts
and above it a hand which does not allow an end.

RETURN TO SILENCE

Hidden in winter, among stopped watches,
awaits own voice to appear of itself
from under the icy surface
—then wanders off, because he's now allowed,
disappears, looks at his own picture in icebergs,
converses with the dead, those who are always here,
behind a cliff, behind shoulders,
dines with them the first silence after everything.

For a time doesn't move, exhausted,
then, again, rises in restlessness
with a horde of boys who can see what is not there,
then maidens with a fragrance of April waters.
Swarms of insects in the sun, barking, cawing of crows.
May scenes on a wide canvas
in front of an empty auditorium.

Then from all explosions returns to his silence,
among the skeletons of watches' half-alive minutes,
into the cold which with a fine hand overgrew the arches.

KARLOVAC PHOENIX

Slowly, always from the beginning
we place our footsteps on the left and right sides
of the streets, a dead spirit lures us into its snare
absorbs the ruins but not the dead
who together stare at us from over there where
they always stood, what can we say before them
we the living who stumble, carry like a precious drop
a bit of life in ourselves, feel after so many days
of emptiness a beginning of an echo in ourselves
and in the whole torn expanse of the city,
the children run by us or are we ourselves still
underage, late roaming takes hold of us but
we see it does not lift a single brick,
laughter overtakes us, and immediately sticks to
until then hidden, unrolled, other laughter
and all the walls of the wounded city become real,
through the windows in still unsafe air blares
loud music from rosy corners of the underground,
a yellow photograph of a horse appears, but
the tame animal really pulls a cart over us too,
hungry for hope, the dust really falls,
gradually other feet also touch the wounded ground,
violently, but behind us so brightly slammed
the doors, and look, after the burst of ingenuous wonders
of renewal of the world, that almost was totally extinguished,
no longer in our deathly recollection but
hearing the bell echo under the ruins
of a vanished chapel, exactly as if nothing had
happened, but everything had happened, and a few of us
dead and alive are heraldic voices of the happy
times that assail like a storm.

CARNIVAL PRINCE

A mask approaches me.
I ask, where to, beauty?
She waves her hand, which can mean
nothing and everything, then disappears in a whirlpool.

I had thought, tonight I will not see her.
Vidrić's *purple eclipse*★ fell upon my mask.
Then I felt a violent wind cutting me
not from the cold but the mad human flesh.

I stopped breathing, again sniffed an evil path.
She called me through the multitude but I could not respond.
My naked hand showed me the way, in vain.
The square tightened-stretched like an accordion.

Masks flew from all sides, unrestrained,
with torches pushing toward the hungry pyre.
"Burn the Prince," I recognized the sweet voice
and passionately embraced the voices.

★Vladimir Vidrić: *Adieu*

MEPHISTO-WALTZ

We are all in the same dance with the same music
which glimmers together with the candles
with white arrows of silvery mirrors
in which ruthlessly grins the one

who with a glance invites to sin.
"Esteemed gentleman from the underground,
you still offer the same contract
for the same price?" He doesn't even

look at me but at the dazzling beauty
I submissively hold in my arms;
with a blue gaze awaits her answer.

In torment I also laugh. And ask
myself: yes or no, and when, and for how long?
but already I hear her dreadful answer.

STORM AT SEA

Sea conversation exists, from sea to sea,
it whispers a lullaby in the ear of the earth.
Blue silence exists which continues the oceans
it seems the universe opens them a door.
Then the music begins from out of blind depths
and each wave is a different harmony that only in a poem
acquires meaning and rises toward the sky.
And the New Moon sails over dark furrows.
The boats seek how to land from the surface
when the Evil One, raging, lights the fire
and throws the whole ocean over its shoulders.
Roar and howl. Laughter and a woman's cry.
That's the sea breaking the Evil One's back
to find again its morning rest.

LUCIFER'S DIARY

In that book of gold and fire, in that
erotic diary of violence, tempting evil,
he searches for the only day of azure, silence.
And immediately, from the other side, whispers
into his all burning auditory canals:
You seek not to find or to backward vomit
flames, to burn the last rags of your thought
of salvation, blissfulness, forgiveness.

Will he discard the list of his crimes?
Suspects there is nothing in his hand, only
continuously delayed beginning. And that possibility
to ask for forgiveness from the One who for long
has not been there. Fear breaks him:
is not the One of whom he mutters has not been there
for long, in his own search of the only day without
a crime? Then, having broken the wish, even more violently
distorting his face, jumps into the highest fire.

BEHIND MY BACK

The one to whom I speak is here but is still
invisible. The words I utter go straight
then turn the corner, swing down a wide street
among daisies that glow even more.
Then I no longer know where they could be,
in what parade, accident, tippling in a tavern,
argument among sparrows and coachmen, perhaps they crawl
into a cellar, sadly asking themselves where are they from,
but the one who incessantly returns us to our senses,
lifts words out of a puddle, they circle the world,
each ruler taking from them a portion,
and here they are with squinting eyes behind my back.
Finally I hear them, but no longer understand.

TIME

Time destroys us with the illusion
that we exist. That we expand like
sweet colonies of ants. We do not see
who comes in our place, who equally
hurries, waves hands, falls into the magic box
of black isolation. Time–fabricator moves
with a drum around its neck and shouts: I am
your only consolation, without me you are again ashes,
in my saddle everyone is beautiful, smart, strong.
Equally, be it good time or bad,
it is tyranny of movement only that in the end
reason does not wake up and open its eyes,
removes the cage around itself and pulls out a sword.
Isn't it the moment someone defend us
from the dragon that vomits seconds, minutes, hours?

SAD SUN

To you also, Sun, they foretold the future,
but where will the prophets be
when you, reticently to sorrow, begin to speak?

Everything will turn upside down.
Our lives will erase and the tough fortresses
which grew against our will.

Time will cowardly wag its little tail
because it will be hit vertically in the middle.

Return a little more, Sun, to your holy place
so I can complete this poem I write in your honour.

Rise in the morning, drop darkness at night
so I can find my verse.

HOME ASSIGNMENT: THE SUN

The sun hides behind the leaves, but poorly.
It's ashamed of its hairiness,
and besides has a large belly.
If it wanted, it could cover the whole sky,
there would be too much of it both up and down,
then one could see what a monster it is.
It never thought of washing its teeth,
cutting off the mustache and beard, thunder of hair.
After all, what is the Sun to us: a blessing to the fields
or a tyrant that pulls us this or that way
by the reins, beats us with a red-hot whip?
I would like once to see tears in its eyes,
hear its birdlike little voice.

DEATH OF A PARROT

When I bought it then at the Bird Market
quite sick, it believed in me.

And when for days I repeated to it
the same words, it looked at me with a knowing
glance, and I was afraid.

When in the end it began to speak
and it was less of a bird, and all the more a cursed
human word.

Many friends visited me again
and moved their head listening to my lost
voice in its beak.

And when I would think of whose soul
moved into its body and what kind of miracles
still await me.

It wanted to tell me something important
but my intellect was not yet ready
for the biggest discoveries.

It did not lose patience and tried
with love; and for it I was
a poor, helpless bird.

When it seriously got sick and no longer
cared to be like a human being.

And at the end when it completely stopped talking
and was only an unbearable pain.

When it expired at the bottom of the cage, again
with love in its eyes, and when between us
any kind of difference disappeared.

(1977)

A KISS OF SOLITUDE

You no longer test speech. Your words
silently pour out of dead passages, on a side,
where senses don't reach. They hardly carry
your seal; if you dared,
you could hear machines as they blindly
produce them. You could discover some workshop,
here, in this body that you guard in yourself,
for long you could go through rooms whose purpose
you don't know, at the end you would bitterly sob.

Without a single sign of self, but still built
into each wall of this sublime ship
which hurries toward its hungry goal. Labour. Roar.
You cover ears with your palms not to hear
anything too closely. Blue laughter
in which is your madness, but without your
exultation. Sweaty you trace after yourself
because all the more firmly you believe that it's in vain;
someone turned you into many of you, among which
not one is any longer you. All together
only barely a recollection of you. Something that will
remain when you leave, to labour, to labour, to labour,
while you were only an inexhaustible dream.

You look around. Sometimes you think you could
even choose. Renounce all that came
later and kneel before the first root.
Or agree to an exchange and accept
riches of someone unknown but still yours.
And thus slowly you are becoming all the more

invisible in a world which you, against your will,
populated too much with your own self.
Your dream is love but only solitude loves you.

(1981)

POST OPERATIONEM

Gentle folk, in those long brown halls
—I freely call them tunnels;
how wouldn't I know: I was a lost
traveller in them, naked on a moving bed

and later under radiant suns
surrounded by green masks—
you exchanged my body,
hardly surviving, but to me a
very dear body in regard to memories
that tie me to it,
even though from all not many remain.

Mine you gave to someone unknown
and his you skillfully planted
onto my soul.

There it is under the covers
all wounded, without a drop of blood.

Take it and give it to the one
who now probably cries after it

and return to me mine,
I have important business with it.
I would like, before it's too late,
to take it to more serene planets.

(March 17, 1987)

129

REVOLT OF THE FLOWERS

First we planted flowers, recreated in the garden
beautiful pictures of Baroque masters, those called
Happy Danes, and then let them, not without curiosity,
and not without silent madness, to grow
alone, to wrestle from spring to autumn with
the weeds. We matured, became wicked.
We hesitated. Is it wiser to reject obedience
to knowledge, as a child would, offended,
sit in the middle of a puddle in the street, or on its face,
with so many suppressed reasons, laughingly mock?
Let those born fight! Nettle's ridicule laughs because
it will live even when it is senseless.
It will procreate, grow, expand out of its own destruction.

And so flower beauties at first sadly
died. As if their survival depends only
on goodwill. At night they would timidly knock on the door,
windows. Then knocked softer, because like all other
cowards quickly anticipated the real meaning of the game
that hit them. Did they then contemplate
a revolt? Selected perhaps their captain?
In late hours forged weapons? Because all these roses,
small hedges, orchids, endured. They are no longer beautiful,
neither are the colours on their petals evenly
arranged. Under the leaves, flowers, they hide
thorns, poisons, teeth, but they grow, all the more
raising their heads. Soon they will again knock
on the door, but with a different purpose.

(1988)

COURT'S FOOL
(The king speaks)

How funny is our court's fool: continuously
with an ear to the door. Needs to know everything poor
creature, see everything. If you come out into the hall at night,
you will likely meet him; he hurries because a new thought
came to him. He wants by force
to change the world. To put things in better
order. Eliminate injustice. He believes he knows
what is and where is the world. If he begins hard-
headed to really arrange it, the world will fall
on his and our heads. He does not know
that the world, be it this or that, hangs by a thread.
If he begins to move things and put them
in the order his head demands, soon we will
remain with nothing. Things will plot
against us. Demand satisfaction.
As far as justice is concerned, is it not often
worse than injustice? Poor fool, return
to your room and try to sleep. Only in sleep
is it worth being concerned about the world.

(1988)

TREES

The trees go first, announcing spring.
They enter through the windows, sit at the table,
sometimes completely alone, in thought,
as if they remember everything. Then the household
with a shout burst through the door, sit around,
as the trees piously cut their bread.

Now I no longer see them in homes.
They are kept in cages at the Botanical
Garden. They are not at the shores of rivers,
among bathers, and when everyone leaves,
they no longer hold a dark night watch. (Here
with them were the birds, silent while people passed,
and when gone, they would turn a page in a book
and their chirping became clear speech.)

Now many trees are deep below the horizon.
They await their sisters and brothers to get out of a noose.
Only steel thunder of the axe can be heard.
Humming of the saw which alone moves from tree to tree.
And when all find themselves on the same side of the hill
the balance of the world will change its proportions.

A WHIRL

The mind comes late. It's delayed by infinite
music, wants to sing in Monteverdi
madrigals, play the harpsichord in Bach's
Well-Tempered Clavier. Drink a jug of
Opolo in a garden restaurant. Embrace
love across all seas and mountain
ranges, never to arrive at the end.

The body on the contrary rushes, with a steel cable
ties the beginning and the end. From weakness falls
onto its emaciated palm which draws for it a picture
of destiny. It forgets. Howls at others
without seeing it walks with them. Buries a pernicious
thought in a secret place for which it then
frantically looks praying not to find it.

The soul at departure watches all this
from the fence. Heavenly whirl is already pulling it.
It asks itself what out of everything can it take:
love which is counterbalance among things,
a pernicious thought which straightens its bones,
a deed which unites the fools.
And it doesn't suspect the doors above are locked.

THE CHAPEL OF ST. MARY OF THE SNOW

The chapel, a castle of sugar
under the old city of Dubrovnik...
Around it rings of trees
which urge me to approach it
and pull the bell's rope
announcing to all I am here.

It's the same, even if it snowed.
A narrow path small wreath of prayers.
Footsteps stop in front of It
and want to be planted here.
A voice in the wind whispers: "Go farther.
Do not forget to return."

A priest enters and disappears
among the books. Words of deep gold
lead me out of darkness into glitter, speak
of the unknown which soars above us.
It smiles and guards us from ourselves.

Hides the head under a wing.
From the East thunderous roars
that disappear upon waking.
This is only a recollection
of childhood.

(Karlovac 2003)

CHISELLED INTO NOTHINGNESS

I have nothing to say anymore to anyone
but, curiously enough, words once uttered
are small white fires in the same place
and I suspect they never die out.

Words, now already light,
attempts of the soul to manifest itself,
help the trees to continue putting forth leaves
and there is no fear of those with hatchets.

In harmony with invisible air
which is equally oppressed but remains
love conversations of long ago can again be heard
if you go far into the carousel of deep colours.

And you are still under the same umbrella
on a bench which hides in the greenery.
There is no danger you are nowhere
each word of yours is chiselled into nothingness
which for many is an illusion but it
returns me to the same embraces.

(Korana Park, Karlovac 2003)

THE CROATIAN TONGUE
for grandson Luka

The tongue you don't know until
  your mouth is set,
burns in you, expands in a narrow
  space
and many splits before breaking
  silence
throwing to the wind, like a flower,
  thousands of seeds.

Then in Croatian murmur grasses,
  the sea and the shore.
I really heard a forest whisper
  in silence
begging me to save it from fire.
And grass would sing to me in Croatian
  so I could easily fall asleep.

We sit around the table and speak
  in that holy tongue,
and sense as around us open
  doors
at which advances the light of the world
that is hidden in the goodness
  of the tongue.

CARNIVAL OF ANIMALS

I would change my mask, says the louse,
for one of a larger beast,
only so I don't recognize myself.
A sad centipede would rather be a lightning bug.
On its nose they stuck a semblance of a cow's
and its mooing was heard long into the night.
A tipsy wheel spins
around a gadfly with an elephant's mask.
"I didn't want that," it cries.
"Paid fairly for a mask of an ape."
Grimacing devil doesn't answer:
he knew how many gadflies had changed masks.
Even the king came once,
but his rattle continuously kept falling.

KEYS TO NAMES AND PLACES

Botanički vrt
  Botanical Garden in Zagreb, founded in 1889 and opened in 1891.

Dobra
  One of the four rivers in Karlovac.

Dolac
  Farmers' market located in Gornji Grad (Upper Town) Medveščak, city
  district of Zagreb, Croatia. It is located just above the main city square,
  Ban Josip Jelačić Square.

Dubrovnik
  Known as the "Pearl of the Adriatic," Dubrovnik is a walled city on the
  Adriatic Sea coast of the extreme south of Croatia. Damaged by an earth-
  quake and again in the 1990s by armed conflict, it is now the focus of a
  major restoration program coordinated by UNESCO.

Glagolica
  Glagolitic script is the oldest known Slavic alphabet. It was created in
  the ninth century by Saint Cyril, a Byzantine monk. He and Saint
  Methodius were sent to spread Christianity among the Slavs.

Gornji grad
  Upper Town, a part of the historical core of today's Zagreb, once known
  as Gradec, then Grič.

Gubčeva zvijezda
  A street in Zagreb's Upper Town.

Ilica

Ilica is one of the largest streets in Zagreb and the most expensive residential street in the city. It runs from Ban Josip Jelačić Square to the western entrance to the city; first mentioned in 1431.

Jadransko more

Adriatic Sea, located between Croatia and Italy, with numerous islands along the Croatian coastline.

Kaptol

Part of the historical core of today's city of Zagreb.

Karlovac

The city of Karlovac emerged around a star-shaped Renaissance fortress built against the Ottomans. It is known as the city of parks and a town on four rivers, of which Mrežnica, Korana, and Kupa flow through it, and Dobra is a few kilometres outside the city center.

Korana

One of the four rivers in Karlovac.

Kupa

One of the four rivers in Karlovac.

Kvaternikov Trg

Also known as Kvatrić Market. It is an outdoor market.

Manduševac

A fountain on Zagreb Central Square of Ban Josip Jelačić. In the past it was a natural source which legends tie to the founding of the city.

Medveščak

Gornji Grad (Upper Town), a district of Zagreb, located in the central part of the city.

Mirogoj

A cemetery park considered to be among the more noteworthy landmarks in the city of Zagreb.

Mrežnica

One of the four rivers in Karlovac.

Nama

An acronym for Narodni magazin (National store), a retail store at the beginning of Ilica street off Ban Josip Jelačić Square.

Nizozemci

West Hollanders, Netherlanders, Dutch.

Pag

The fifth largest island in the North Dalmatian Archipelago, Croatia.

Phoenix

Egyptian myth – a beautiful, lone bird which lived in the Arabian desert from 500-600 years and then consumed itself in fire, rising renewed from the ashes to start another long life. A symbol of immortality.

Split

Split is the second-largest city in Croatia and the largest in the region of Dalmatia.

Tuškanac

A neighbourhood located in Gornji Grad – Medveščak city District of Zagreb, Croatia. It is best known for its parks and the Tuškanac cinema.

Vladimir Vidrić

A Croatian poet who lived from 1875 to 1909. He is considered one of the major figures of the Croatian Secessionist movement.

Vltava

A river in central Czech Republic which runs through Prague.

Zagreb

Capital and the largest city of the Republic of Croatia. It is located in the northwest of the country, along the Sava River, with a population of over one million. The name "Zagreb" is mentioned for the first time in 1094 at the founding of the Zagreb diocese of Kaptol.

Zrinjevac

Colloquial term for Nikola Šubić Zrinski Square – the oldest of seven city park-squares in Donji Grad (Lower Town), the central part of Zagreb, named in 1866.

BIOGRAPHICAL NOTES

Slavko Mihalić (1928-2007) is one of the giants in Croatian literature of the second half of the twentieth century. He was born in 1928 in Karlovac, Croatia, where he finished high school and then moved to Zagreb where he worked for a newspaper and published his first book of poetry, *Komorna muzika (Chamber Music)* in 1954. During the course of his life, he worked as an anthologist, publisher, editor, critic, writer for children, authored over twenty books of poetry, and established several literary journals and the literary review *Most (Bridge)*, which brought Croatian literature to international readers. In this endeavour he attracted translators and himself translated from several Slavic languages, as well as from the Italian, English, and German. His main goal has always been to promote literature. Translated into major world languages, Slavko Mihalić is a recipient of numerous literary awards, among them Tin Ujević, City of Zagreb, Matica hrvatska, Miroslav Krleža, Goranov vijenac, Vladimir Nazor and others.

Dasha C. Nisula completed her Ph.D. degree in Comparative Literature at the University of Southern California. She began teaching at USC, then at Baylor University, and at Western Michigan University, where she obtained full Professorship with a Distinguished Teaching Award. For most of her career she has been teaching Russian and Croatian languages, literature, and culture, as well as translating poetry and short stories from these languages. She is author of four books, numerous articles, reviews, and translations which have appeared in *An Anthology of South Slavic Literatures*, and in literary journals as *Modern Poetry in Translation*, *Southwestern Review*, *International Poetry Review*, and *Massachusetts Review* among others. A member of the American Literary Translators Association, she lives and works in Kalamazoo, Michigan.

ACKNOWLEDGEMENTS

My thanks go to the family of Slavko Mihalić, sons Tomislav and Zlatko Mihalić, for giving me permission to translate and publish poetry by their father. I am sure that these poems will continue to inspire Croatian readers and, no doubt, will be appreciated by English-speaking readers around the world.

Thanks to Elizabeth Marquart, B.M., for her patience in reading first translations of these poems and offering insights and suggestions, as well as to Dillon Dolby, B.A., for his excellent technical assistance with this project. My gratitude goes to Inez Bareza, M.S., whose knowledge of some special expressions was indispensable to my understanding of the original text. And my special thanks go to Roxanne Panicacci, M.D., Ph.D., for her suggestions on the final draft of the manuscript.

Three poems included in this selection have previously appeared in print. I am grateful to acknowledge *Massachusetts Review* for taking interest in publishing "Mozart's Magic Coach" in their Winter 2016 The Music Issue, Vol. LVII, No. 4, p. 766, "Coffee Cantata" in their Fall 2017 issue, Vol. LVIII, No. 3, p. 509 and "Boy with a Ball" in the Spring 2019 issue, Vol. LX, No. 1, p. 78, as well as *Journal of Ophthalmology* for publishing "The Eye" in their November 2016 issue, Vol. 171, pp. 157-158.

I also wish to thank Chair Lynde-Recchia, Department of World Languages and Literatures, Dean Koetsky of the College of Arts and Sciences, and Provost Stapleton at Western Michigan University in Kalamazoo, Michigan, for their support of my work. And finally, I am grateful to the publisher, Michael Callaghan, for his continued interest in this project.

D. C. N.

PARTIAL BIBLIOGRAPHY

Komorna muzika / Chamber Music. Zagreb: Lykos, 1954.

Put u nepostojanje / Road to Nonexistence. Zagreb: Lykos, 1956.

Početak zaborava / Beginning of Oblivion. Zagreb: Zora, 1957.

Darežljivo progonstvo / Generous Exile. Zagreb: Lykos, 1959.

Godišnja doba / Seasons of the Year. Zagreb: s.n., 1961.

Ljubav za stvarnu zemlju / Love for a Real Homeland. Zagreb: Zora, 1964.

Jezero / Lake. Beograd: Prosveta, 1966.

Posljednja večera / The Last Supper. Zagreb: Kolo, 1969/1970.

Vrt crnih jabuka / Orchard of Black Apples. Zagreb: Studentski centar Sveučilišta, 1972.

Klopka za uspomene / Trap for Memories. Zagreb: Znanje, 1977.

Pohvala praznom džepu / In Praise of an Empty Pocket. Zagreb: Liber, 1981.

Tihe lomače / Silent Stakes. Zagreb: Naprijed, 1985.

Iskorak / Out of Step. Zagreb: Naprijed, 1987.

Ispitivanje tišine / Examination of Silence: Mozart's Magic Coach. Ljubljana-Zagreb: Mladinska knjiga, 1990.

Zavodnička šuma / Seductive Forest. Zagreb: Naklada MD, 1992.

Baršunasta žena / Velvety Woman. Zagreb: Meander, 1993.

Karlova kičdiptih / Karlovac Diptych. Matica hrvatska Karlovac, 1995.

Približavanje oluje / Approaching Storm. Zagreb: Školska knjiga, 1996.

Pandorina kutija / Pandora's Box. Zagreb: Matica hrvatska, 1997.

Akordeon / Accordion. Zagreb: Društvo hrvatskih književnika, 2000.

Močvara / Marsh. Zagreb: Ljevak, 2004.

AWARDS

Association of Croatian Writers, 1957
for *Put u nepostojanje / Road to Nonexistence* (1956)

City of Zagreb, 1962
for *Godišnja doba / Seasons of the Year* (1961)

Matica hrvatska, 1967
for *Izabrane pjesme / Selected Poems* (1966)

City of Zagreb, 1970
for *Posljednja večera / The Last Supper* (1969)

"Ivana Brlić Mažuranić," 1976
for *Petrica Kerempuh*, Prose (1975)

"Tin Ujević," 1982
for *Pohvala praznom džepu / In Praise of an Empty Pocket* (1981)

"Zmaj"/"Fund Miroslav Krleža," 1987
for *Tihe lomače / Silent Stakes* (1985)

"Goranov vijenac"/Goran Wreath, 1990
for *Izabrane pjesme / Selected Poems* (1988)

"Vladimir Nazor," 1993
for *Zavodnička šuma / Seductive Forest* (1992)

"Vladimir Nazor," 1996
for Lifetime Achievement

"Visoka žuta žita"/Povelja, 1997
for Continuous Contribution to Croatian Literature

"Ivan Goran Kovačić"/"Vjesnik," 1998
for *Pandorina kutija / Pandora's Box* (1997)

"Dobrojutro, more"/Podstrana, 1999
for Continuous Contribution to Croatian Literature

"Maslinov vijenac"/Olive Wreath, 1999
for Poetry Achievement, Selce, Island of Brač

Vilenica, Association of Slovenian Writers, 2000
Central-European Literary Award

Zlatni vijenac/Golden Wreath, 2002
Struga Poetry Evenings, Struga, Macedonia; Association of
    Macedonian Writers

ALPHABETICAL INDEX OF TITLES